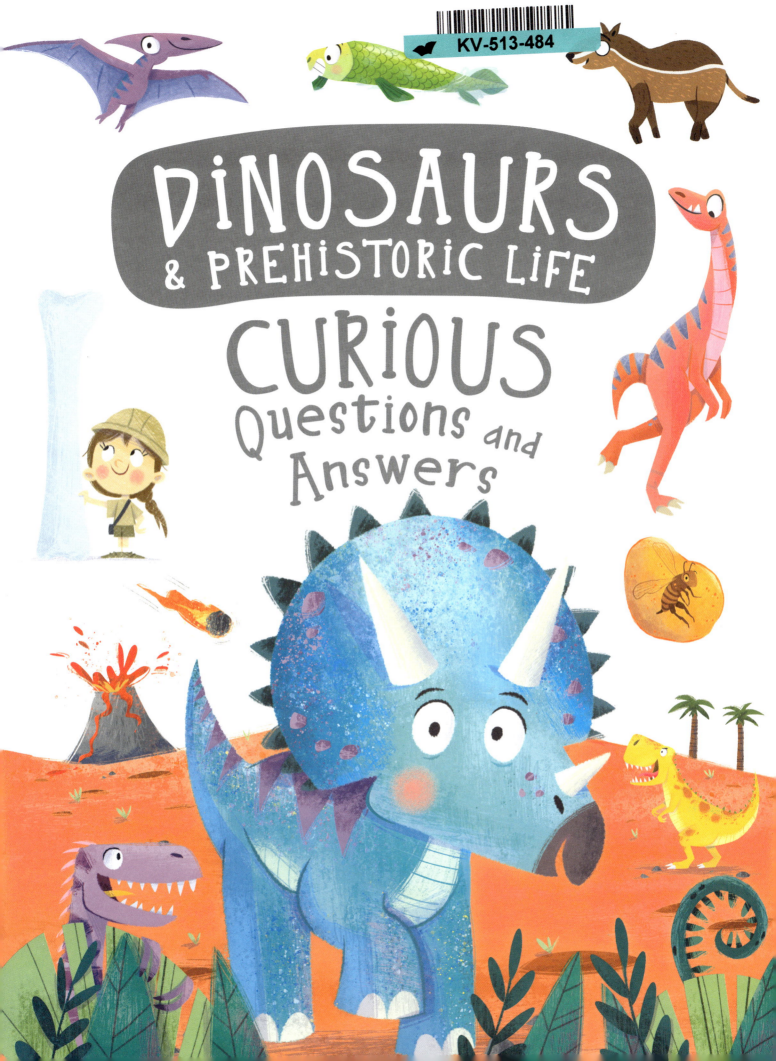

DINOSAURS
& PREHISTORIC LIFE

CURIOUS
Questions and Answers

DINOSAURS & PREHISTORIC LIFE

CURIOUS Questions and Answers

Words by Camilla de la Bédoyère and Philip Steele

Illustrations by Leire Martín, Pauline Gregory and Jack Viant

MILES KELLY

First published in 2022 by Miles Kelly Publishing Ltd
Harding's Barn, Bardfield End Green, Thaxted, Essex, CM6 3PX, UK

Copyright © Miles Kelly Publishing Ltd 2022

2 4 6 8 10 9 7 5 3

Publishing Director Belinda Gallagher
Creative Director Jo Cowan
Editorial Director Rosie Neave
Editors Fran Bromage, Sarah Carpenter
Designers Joe Jones, Simon Lee, Emily Stalley
Image Manager Liberty Newton
Production Jennifer Brunwin
Reprographics Stephan Davis
Assets Lorraine King

Cover Artist Pipi Sposito @ Advocate Art

ISBN 978-1-78989-241-3

Printed in China

British Library Cataloguing-in-Publication Data
A catalogue record for this book is available from the British Library

Made with paper from a sustainable forest

www.mileskelly.net

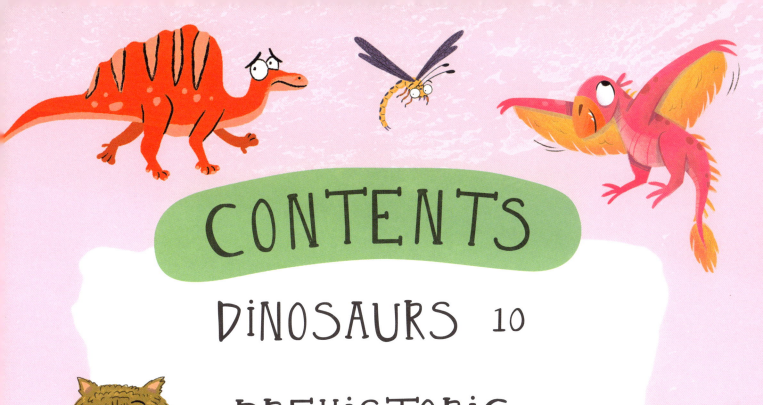

CONTENTS

10

DINOSAURS

When did dinosaurs live?

The first dinosaurs lived about 240 million years ago, long before there were people. Dinosaurs evolved from other animals called dinosauromorphs. They were cat-sized reptiles.

i'm a dinosauromorph. When an animal evolves it changes over time, so it can survive in a changing world.

i'm one of the first dinosaurs. i lived about 230 million years ago.

Herrerasaurus

Tarbosaurus

i'm one of the last dinosaurs. i roamed the planet 70 million years ago.

Were all dinosaurs huge?

Dinosaurs came in all shapes and sizes. The largest ones were called titanosaurs. They were more than 20 metres long and weighed as much as six elephants!

I'm one of the biggest dinosaurs ever. Can you guess where in the world I came from?

Argentinosaurus

This tiny terror is Microraptor. It is just 40–60 centimetres long

Being small helps me to glide from trees.

Where did they live?

The first dinosaurs lived on Pangaea — a single, giant slab of land. The world was very hot and dry and there was just one ocean called Panthalassa. Dinosaurs could walk all the way from the North Pole to the South Pole. We call this time in Earth's history the Triassic.

PANGAEA

Who would be at a dino party?

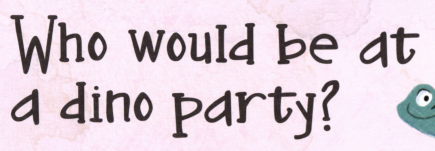

Dinosaurs were reptiles, so they might invite other reptiles. These baby *Maiasaura* have just hatched, so they are sharing their birthday party. Can you spot which guests are not dinosaurs?

Maiasaura

Who looked after the babies?

Maiasaura mums took good care of their nests, eggs and young. They protected them from hungry Troodon.

Watch out kids, that hungry Troodon has its big eyes on you!

Troodon was an intelligent dinosaur with big eyes and sharp claws

Why do dinos have such strange names?

Dinosaur names are often made up of more than one word. Put together, the words tell us more about the dinosaur.

Carcharodontosaurus shark-tooth-lizard

Tyrannosaurus rex tyrant-lizard-king

Guanlong crown-dragon

Maiasaura good mother-lizard

Triceratops three-horned-face

Torosaurus bull-lizard

Mei long sleeping-dragon

Hey, who is Tyrannosaurus rex?

Mei long was covered in bird-like feathers and may have been very colourful

Did dinosaurs have fur?

No, dinosaurs didn't have fur but many of them had feathers. The feathers were often fluffy, but some dinosaurs grew long feathers, like modern birds. Fuzzy, fluffy feathers kept dinosaurs warm.

Yutyrannus was up to 9 metres long and covered in fuzzy feathers

15

Did you know?

A fully-grown *T rex* was **longer** and **heavier** than a bus and its skull was so heavy you'd need a forklift truck to pick it up.

In 1824 **Megalosaurus** was the first dinosaur to be named. When its thighbone was dug up people thought it belonged to a human giant!

Meat-eating dinosaurs had long, curved, sharp teeth.

Titanosaurs were huge, long-necked dinosaurs but they were not the largest animals to ever live. The **blue whale**, which lives in our oceans today, wins that prize.

Plant-eaters had peg-like or spoon-shaped teeth.

All dinos could **walk**, some of them could **swim** and others – like *Microraptor* – could **glide** between trees.

Dinosaurs didn't have **kneecaps**, but no one knows why!

T rex and *Tarbosaurus* might have made good **ballet dancers** – they balanced beautifully on their tiptoes!

Ichthyosaurs were fast-swimming reptiles that lived in the sea. They looked like whales or dolphins, but were related to **snakes** and **lizards**.

Which dinosaurs had the longest necks?

Mamenchisaurus had a long, thin neck that was 12 metres in length

Mamenchisaurus

Sauropods were a group of huge dinosaurs with very long necks, like *Brachiosaurus*. Having a long neck meant that sauropods could reach high up into trees to eat leaves. They might spend all day eating.

Brachiosaurus

Parasaurolophus

Could dinosaurs roaaarr?

No one knows what sounds dinosaurs made. They may have roared, growled, chirped, tweeted — or made no sounds at all. *Parasaurolophus* had a long, hollow crest on its head. It may have blown air through the crest to make honking sounds — like a trumpet!

18

Diplodocus

Diplodocus *had a long, bendy tail too, which it used to wallop other dinosaurs.*

Do you think I'm handsome?

Oviraptor

Some dinosaurs liked to look good! Horns, frills, head plates and colourful feathers or skin may have all helped male dinosaurs look attractive to female ones.

Who was king of the dinosaurs?

Look out! Here comes *Tyrannosaurus rex* — king of the dinosaurs. *T rex* was a massive 13 metres long and weighed about 7 tonnes — that makes it one of the biggest meat-eaters that's ever lived on land, in the whole history of the planet!

T rex may have hunted in groups. A pack of them would have been a terrifying sight for a Triceratops like me!

Yikes!

How scary was a T rex?

T rex was one of the scariest dinosaurs to ever live. It was a huge, fearsome, powerful hunter that preyed on other big dinosaurs. It could bite its prey so hard it snapped bones.

Sharp claws on hands and feet

When did T rex live?

T rex lived at the end of the Cretaceous Period, 68 to 66 million years ago. Scientists have so far found about 50 skeletons of T rex in North America.

Thick, scaly skin with fuzzy feathers sticking out between the scales

Why are my hands so tiny?

T rex had small arms and hands but they were very strong, and had nasty claws. T rex may have gripped prey close to its chest as it sank its razor-sharp teeth into the flesh.

Each eyeball was the size of a grapefruit

Great sense of smell, and good eyesight.

Huge jaws were packed with long, razor-sharp teeth

How many?

3

The number of claws *Therizinosaurus* had on each hand — the longest was 71 centimetres long! It probably used its claws to grab branches and pull leaves to its mouth.

10

The size in centimetres of the smallest known dinosaur eggs. The biggest were 30 centimetres long — twice as big as an ostrich egg.

50

The number of new species of dinosaur being discovered every year.

In 1905 the bones of a *T rex* were put on display in a museum for the first time. Scientists thought they were just **8 million** years old!

T rex could run at speeds of about **30** kilometres an hour — that's faster than an elephant but much slower than a racehorse.

Most dinos probably grew quickly and died before they reached the age of

30.

The world was about **6°** Celsius hotter during the Cretaceous than it is today. The hot, steamy weather meant that lush forests could grow as far as the North Pole!

19 The number of bones in the neck of Mamenchisaurus – more than any dinosaur discovered so far.

2 The weight in kilograms that a 10-year-old *T rex* would have gained every day! A newly hatched *T rex* would have been the size of pigeon, but it grew super fast.

The Jurassic Period lasted **55 million** years. Then Pangaea began to break up into big chunks of land called continents.

How did dinosaurs defend themselves?

Many plant-eating dinosaurs had bony armour to protect them from attack. Thick slabs of bone, plates, scales, spikes and bony bumps all helped ankylosaurs fend off the razor-sharp claws and dagger-like teeth of meat-eating dinosaurs.

Ankylosaurus

Why is there a big club on your tail?

Smash!

I'm an ankylosaur from the Late Cretaceous. I have a huge club on the end of my tail and it's very useful for walloping anything that attacks me — like that T rex over there!

What did dinosaurs eat?

Some dinosaurs hunted animals to eat, other dinosaurs ate plants, and some ate whatever they could find!

I'm fully armed with slashing, gripping claws and jaws lined with razor-sharp teeth. I'm fast, smart... and hungry for meat!

Raptors, like Deinonychus, were light on their feet and super speedy.

Sauropelta

I eat plants. My body is covered in bony plates and spikes that make it difficult for Deinonychus to attack me!

How much did T rex eat?

Yum!

T rex was a hungry beast that needed about 110 kilograms of meat a day. That's more than 1000 burgers!

Plant-eaters like me graze on low-growing plants and leaves. Even our teeth are shaped like leaves!

I look like an ostrich with my long legs, feathers and toothless beak. I mostly peck at bugs, lizards and other small animals.

Deinonychus

Ornithomimus

How fast could a dinosaur run?

Plant-eating dinosaurs were slow movers, but most predator dinosaurs needed speed to hunt and catch their prey.

Ornithomimus was one of the fastest dinosaurs, with top speeds of 35 kilometres an hour or more.

27

Could dinosaurs fly?

Yes, and they still do! Flying dinosaurs are all around us. We call them birds.

Over a long time, some dinosaurs began to develop bird-like bodies with wings and feathers. By 150 million years ago, the first birds had appeared. That means all birds are actually dinosaurs!

What was the first bird called?

Archaeopteryx — that's me! I have teeth, claws on my wings and a long, bony tail. I can climb, run, glide and even fly a little.

I lived 130 million years ago. I could glide between trees and flap my wings.

Microraptor

Quetzalcoatlus

I'm a giant pterosaur. I have a wingspan of 12 metres and I'm one of the biggest animals to ever fly – one of my feet is bigger than a human's leg!

What is a pterosaur?

Pterosaurs were flying reptiles that lived at the same time as the dinosaurs. Their wings were made of thin skin, spread out between the bones in their arms and fingers, and they were superb flyers.

Would you rather?

Have a **Maiasaura** or **Majungatholus** for a mum? Scientists think that Majungatholus may have eaten members of its own family!

Fight a T rex or **fly** with a pterosaur?

Be a **fast-running** Gallimimus or a **slow-moving** Stegosaurus?

Have **teeth** like T rex or a **neck** like Supersaurus? You'd either need a very big toothbrush, or a very long scarf!

If you had the body of a sauropod would you use your long tail to **splash** in water, or let people **slide** down it?

Be as **big** as Brachiosaurus or as **small** as Microraptor?

Be covered in a coat of **soft, fluffy feathers** or have **scary horns** growing on your face?

Have tea with a *Tarbosaurus*, **cuddle** a *Carcharodontosaurus* or **stroke** a *Stegosaurus*?

How could sauropods grow so big?

Sauropods were giant plant-eaters. They had big bones and huge muscles to move their bodies. They also had holes and air sacs in their bones, which kept them light. Without these, sauropods would have been even heavier!

Could a dinosaur crush a car?

Argentinosaurus weighed over 60 tonnes. If it sat on a car, it could crush it in an instant! *T rex* had one of the most powerful bites of any animal ever known. It could have crushed a car in its mighty jaws!

Crunch!

Brachiosaurus

I am three times taller than a giraffe!

How did dinosaurs kill their prey?

They were equipped with some lethal weapons! Claws, jaws, teeth and tails could all be used to injure, catch or kill other animals. Raptors had long, curved claws on their feet for slashing and slicing.

What happened to the dinosaurs?

After more than 150 million years of ruling the world, disaster struck the dinosaurs. An enormous space rock, called an asteroid, smashed into Earth.

How did Earth change?

It turned cold and dark, and there was very little food because plants couldn't grow. Over the next few thousand years, most types of animals, including the dinosaurs, went extinct.

The dinosaurs began to die, along with many other animals.

The asteroid hit Earth with the explosive force of a billion giant bombs.

There were giant waves, floods and burning winds before dark clouds of dust filled the sky.

Are the dinosaurs still alive?

Yes they are! Birds belong to the dinosaur family, and some survived the asteroid, along with other animals. Today, more than 10,000 different types of bird live all over the world.

Eagles have sharp claws and beaks like many dinosaurs did.

Huge, flightless terror birds lived in South America about two million years ago.

Can you believe I'm a dinosaur? RAAA!

Ducks, geese and chickens are dinosaur relatives.

Who collects dino poo?

① This dinosaur died and its soft parts rotted away.

We do! We're palaeontologists (say: pal-ee-on-tol-oh-jists). We look for the remains of animals that lived long ago.

② Its bones were covered in sand or mud.

What's a fossil?

A fossil is the remains of an animal that has turned to stone over millions of years.

We look at fossils of bones and footprints. Fossil poo helps us to work out what dinosaurs ate.

Where can I find dinosaurs?

Lots of museums have dinosaur fossils you can look at. They are being dug up all over the world, from the USA to China! Mudstone, sandstone and limestone are all good rocks in which to find fossils.

Whose tooth is that?

It's a fossilized tooth from a Trex! Each adult had 50 massive teeth and they could grow new ones if the old ones fell out or broke.

 ③

Over time, the bones were buried by more sand or mud and turned to stone – they have been fossilized.

 My bones are revealed when land erodes (wears away).

A compendium of questions

What was the biggest scary dinosaur to ever live?

It may have been the super scary *Spinosaurus*. It was probably longer and heavier than *T rex*, and its huge head had crocodile-like jaws lined with teeth.

Why did Brachiosaurus eat stones?

Like many reptiles, *Brachiosaurus* probably swallowed stones to help grind up tough plant food in its stomach.

Crunch!

There's plenty more where we came from!

How many types of dinosaur are there?

About 2000 types have been found and named so far, but there are plenty more to discover.

Were dinosaurs clever?

Some were! *Troodon* had a big brain for its size. It was smarter than a turtle but not as clever as a parrot.

On your marks, get set, GO!

Could I out-run a Velociraptor?

No! *Velociraptor* could reach speeds of 35 kilometres an hour. Few animals could escape those razor-sharp claws!

I wasn't a strict vegetarian, and quite often ate fish for dinner!

Which dino could fish?

Deinocheirus could. It had long arms and sharp claws. It may have lurked around rivers to grab a fishy meal or reached high into trees to pick fruit.

Were pterosaurs flying dinosaurs?

Pterosaurs could fly but they were not dinosaurs. They belonged to a group of reptiles that appeared before the first dinosaurs.

Which dinosaur loved stinky smells?

Tarbosaurus was a hunter, but also ate dead animals that it found by following the stench of rotting flesh.

i HERD you needed a friend to lean on.

Were any dinosaurs friendly?

Some dinosaurs, like *Iguanodon*, probably lived peacefully in herds. *T rex* might have hunted in packs, but was probably not friendly!

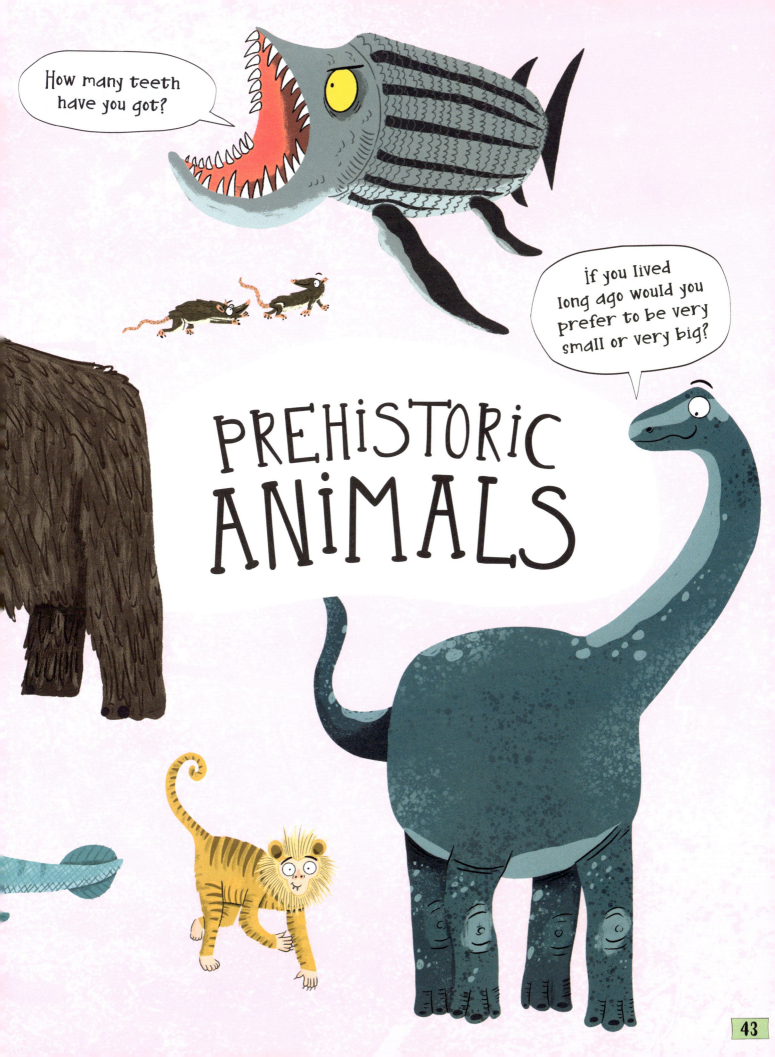

PREHISTORIC ANIMALS

43

When did life begin?

The Earth was formed 4.5 billion years ago, but it took the first 4 billion years for animals to appear. They were small, slithering sea creatures, but over time, millions of other animals appeared.

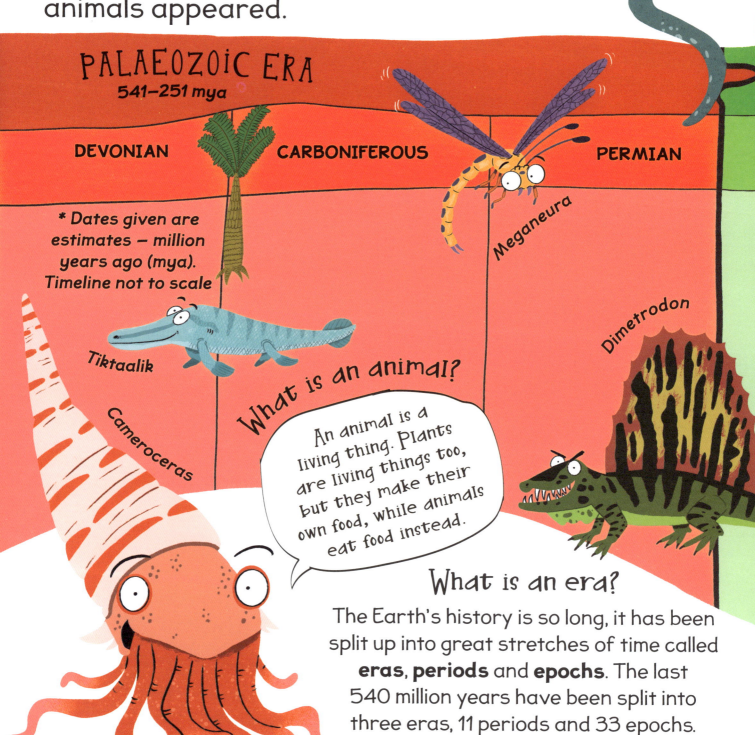

PALAEOZOIC ERA
541–251 mya

DEVONIAN

CARBONIFEROUS

PERMIAN

* Dates given are estimates – million years ago (mya). Timeline not to scale

Meganeura

Dimetrodon

Tiktaalik

Cameroceras

What is an animal?

An animal is a living thing. Plants are living things too, but they make their own food, while animals eat food instead.

What is an era?

The Earth's history is so long, it has been split up into great stretches of time called **eras, periods** and **epochs**. The last 540 million years have been split into three eras, 11 periods and 33 epochs.

Patagotitan

What does prehistoric mean?

Anything that is prehistoric lived, or happened, before humans were able to write about it.

Woolly mammoth

MESOZOIC ERA
251–66 mya

Morganucodon

CENOZOIC ERA
66 mya–present

TRIASSIC	JURASSIC	CRETACEOUS	PALAEOGENE	NEOGENE	QUATERNARY

Archaeopteryx

66 mya
Dinosaurs died out

Why do epochs end?

2.6 mya
Ice Age

First human

The end of each epoch, period or era is usually marked by a big change in the world, such as climate change or sudden extinctions.

Compsognathus

Triceratops

Palaeocene	Eocene	Oligocene	Miocene	Pliocene	Pleistocene	Holocene

The longest period of time was the Cretaceous, which lasted 80 million years

We are in the Holocene epoch of the Quaternary Period

Where are they all now?

If prehistoric animals ran out of food, or the planet got too hot or too cold for them, they died out and went extinct. Some prehistoric animals survived by slowly changing and adapting to new conditions. This is called evolution.

Lots of animals, like dinosaurs, died out at the end of the Cretaceous Period when a massive meteorite hit the planet.

What is a fossil?

A fossil is the remains of a long-dead animal or plant that has been turned into stone.

1 A dead animal is buried in mud, stones or sand.

2 Over a long time, hard body parts, such as shells, bones, teeth and claws are turned into stone.

3 People dig up the fossils to study them.

Which fish walked out of the sea?

Lobe-finned fish, like *Tiktaalik* did! They had strong leg-like fins, which they could use to swim or walk. *Tiktaalik* had lungs and gills, so it could breathe under water or in air.

We evolved to become tetrapods – the group of animals that live on land and walk on four legs.

Tiktaalik

We lived in the sea 400 mya and went extinct at the same time as the dinosaurs.

Ammonite

Dickinsonia

What's that blob of jelly?

Dickinsonia lived on the seabed, about 550 mya. It grew up to 80 centimetres long!

Did you know?

Pterosaurs were **NOT birds** – they were reptiles. Some of them lived at the same time as the first birds.

They had **leathery wings** that were attached to their hand bones and **freaky fourth fingers** that were extra long!

Pterosaur means '**lizard with wings**' and, like the dinosaurs, they all died out 66 mya.

The **largest** pterosaur was Quetzalcoatlus. It was the size of a **small plane**, and the largest animal ever known to fly.

Yikes!

The **smallest** pterosaurs were no bigger than a **sparrow**!

Most pterosaurs had teeth and **long tails**, but evolved to be toothless, with **short tails**.

The first pterosaur **fossils** were found around 1780. Scientists thought it might be a type of **bat**.

A fancy **head crest** was very important to attract a mate.

Squeak!

While most pterosaurs hunted fish, bugs, birds and other **animals**, *Tapejara*, probably ate **fruit and nuts**.

Yuck!

Although these quirky creatures were **reptiles**, like lizards, some had a fuzzy, **feathery layer** to keep them warm.

Was this mega-shrimp just a wimp?

Archelon

Anomalocaris

I'll grow up to be the size of a small car.

I was a metre long and had an armour-plated mouth.

Why are baby sea turtles super speedy?

They need speed to escape hungry hunters! Long ago, little ancient Archelons had to scuttle from the beach, where they hatched, into the sea before being eaten.

Although Anomalocaris looked like a mighty killer, it probably only sucked up defenceless worms and jellyfish, rather than crushing big beasties. What do you think?

Which fish got greedy?

Dunkleosteus had bony plates over its body to protect it

Dunkleosteus

Dunkleosteus had sharp bony blades in its mouth to chop prey into huge chunks, but it couldn't chew. It swallowed the chunks whole and if it ate too much, it threw it all up again!

I did, and it made me sick!

Scientists have found balls of fish sick that have turned into fossils.

Which shark was as long as a bus?

Megalodon was the biggest shark to ever live – bigger than a bus – but it was still smaller than a blue whale.

Blue whale

I hunted whales and giant turtles. My teeth were 20 centimetres long!

Megalodon

Who's lost a tooth?

Fossil-hunters love a puzzle! They look at all kinds of fossils — eggs, teeth, footprints and poo, to work out things about the animal they came from.

Smilodon

This huge tusk was a tooth from an ancient elephant called a Deinotherium.

This long tooth came from Smilodon — a big cat, also known as a sabre-toothed tiger.

Fangs 28 centimetres long!

Grew up to 90 centimetres long

Who did this poo?

Fossilized poo is called coprolite. It can tell palaeontologists (people who study fossils) what animals ate.

Why were mammoths woolly?

Woolly mammoths lived during the Ice Age and grew thick fur to keep warm. When they died, their bodies often froze and were buried under thick layers of ice, which preserved them.

Woolly mammoth

Brrr!

Who got stuck in the mud?

Giant babies did! While *Indricotherium* mothers could wade through squelchy mud, their calves could get stuck and die, eventually turning into fossils.

Indricotherium

Mud was great for making footprints, which are called trace fossils

How many?

A sabre-toothed fish's fangs were **6** centimetres long!

A fossilized Elasmosaurus was found with **197** pebbles in its tummy. The pebbles helped to grind up food.

205,000,000 years ago was when the first furry animals evolved.

Andrewsarchus's skull was **1** metre in length – the biggest meat-eating mammal to ever live.

30

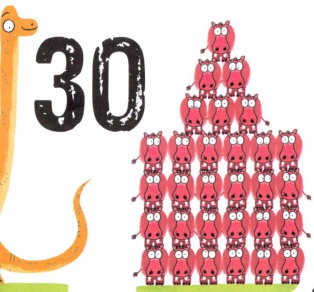

The number of hippos that weigh the same as one *Sauroposeidon*.

1.5

The weight in tonnes of the world's largest ammonite.

The longest dinosaur footprints ever discovered were **170** centimetres long (probably made by giant plant-eating dinosaurs called sauropods).

10

The number of tentacles of a *Cameroceras*. These squid-like creatures had a shell shaped like a giant ice-cream cone!

The length of a Styxosaurus's neck was **6** metres — half of its entire body.

The oldest known fossil of a land-based animal is Kampecaris at **425** million years old.

0

The number of teeth *Shastasaurus* had. It probably sucked up and swallowed jellyfish whole.

Why were bugs so big?

I was a giant plant-eating millipede.

Arthropleura

Long ago there were mega-spiders, massive millipedes, and dragonflies the size of birds! They grew so big because the air contained more oxygen than it does today.

Who had a sting in its tail?

Jaekelopterus was a giant scorpion — twice as big as you! Ancient scorpions preferred watery homes to hunt fish or frogs.

Jaekelopterus

Scientists think Arthropleura could have grown to over 2 metres

Yikes!

I had nasty nipping pincers to grip my prey too!

Who snacked on dinosaurs?

Snap! My favourite meal is a tasty Ouranosaurus!

Sarcosuchus

120 pointy teeth

Massive predators often lurked in shallow, swampy water, waiting for thirsty dinos to come and drink. Sarcosuchus was the length of 10 of you!

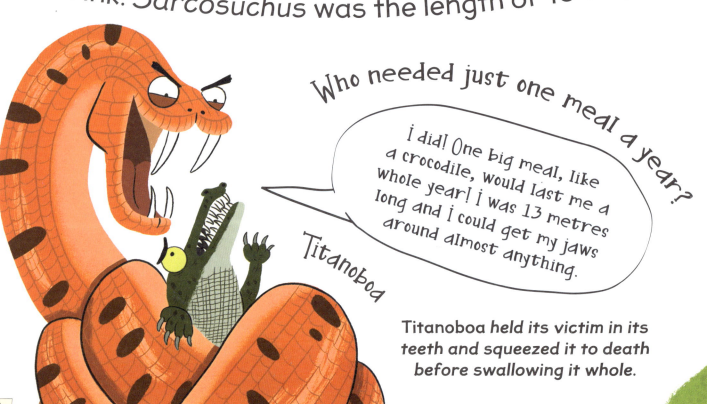

Who needed just one meal a year?

I did! One big meal, like a crocodile, would last me a whole year! I was 13 metres long and I could get my jaws around almost anything.

Titanoboa

Titanoboa held its victim in its teeth and squeezed it to death before swallowing it whole.

What were those claws for?

Although Therizinosaurus had terrifyingly sharp, metre-long curved claws, they were probably only used to strip leaves from trees. They might also have been used to defend itself.

Don't panic – I'm a vegetarian! I'm as big as a Trex, but not as mean.

Therizinosaurus

Did ancient animals need friends?

Hunting together meant that predators like *Hyaenodon* could catch and kill animals bigger than themselves, like *Daeodon*.

Our jaws were strong enough to crush bone!

Daeodon

Hyaenodon

Would you rather?

Be as **snappy** as Xiphactinus or as **prickly** as a prehistoric worm?

Knit a **scarf** for a Diplodocus or take a T rex to the **dentist**?

Hide inside a Glyptodont's shell or try your luck in a **cave** with Arctodus?

Eat **veggies** all day like Megacerops, or dine on dinosaur **eggs** like an ancient snake?

Have **armour**, like Ankylosaurus, or be as **speedy** as Compsognathus?

Be a giant **flying** Haast's eagle, or a tiny **gliding** Microraptor?

Roar!

Have **horns** on your face, like Triceratops, or a **sail** on your back, like Dimetrodon?

Snuggle up with a furry dire wolf or **ride** on a woolly rhino?

Eeek!

Count the **eyes** on Rosamygale or the **legs** on Arthropleura?

Munch, crunch!

We ate lots!

How much could a dinosaur eat?

Titanosaur

Titanosaurs were enormous plant-eating dinosaurs that could eat over 900 kilograms of leaves a day. That's like eating a salad made from 2000 lettuces!

Animals that eat a diet of plants are called herbivores.

Who wallowed in water?

i loved to laze about like a hippo and use my horns to snort and bellow. My legs were made for swimming, so i waddled on land.

Arsinoitherium

Elasmotherium

The horn was used to scare predators.

Were there unicorns in Prehistoric times?

No, but we are sometimes called Siberian unicorns because of our long horns.

Doedicurus

Crash!

Who was built like a tank?

Doedicurus! This mega-armadillo had a tough shell made of more than 1800 bony plates. It also had a big, spiked club on the end of its tail to wallop rivals at mating time.

Could dinosaurs fly?

Many dinosaurs had feathers to keep them warm. Some small, feathered dinosaurs eventually began to fly and evolved to become the first birds, like Archaeopteryx.

Archaeopteryx lived about 150 million years ago.

Elephant bird

Archaeopteryx

We had tiny wings and couldn't fly.

Which bird laid the biggest egg?

The largest bird eggs were laid by elephant birds. One egg would have weighed as much as 150 chicken eggs.

Elephant bird egg

Chicken egg

Confuciusornis

I could only fly short distances between trees.

Moa

We could grow to over 3 metres tall.

Phorusrhacos

This terror bird couldn't fly, but it was fast on its feet

Which bird was a giant?

Many prehistoric birds grew big, but moas were the tallest birds ever known. They lived in New Zealand and were hunted by humans. They probably went extinct 500 years ago.

Did early birds catch worms?

Yes — early birds ate worms, bugs, fish and seeds. Some big birds, known as terror birds, were deadly hunters of larger animals.

Which gentle giant had a bad temper?

i may look like a sleepy sloth, but if you scare me i'll turn nasty!

Megatherium was a sloth as huge as an elephant. It could stand up on its back feet and use its dagger-like claws to slash at attackers.

Megatherium

What's the point in awesome antlers?

Male deer today use their antlers to fight each other at mating time. *Megaloceros* was an ancient deer that did the same thing, with awesome antlers 3 metres across!

Each tip of a deer's antlers is called a point

Antlers are made of bone.

Megaloceros

Which bulky beast had babies the size of jellybeans?

I did! I'm over 2 metres tall but my tiny baby, called a joey, is hiding in my pouch.

Who had massive feet?

This giant orangutan, *Gigantopithecus*, must have had enormous feet, but so far the only fossils found have been teeth and jawbones.

Gigantopithecus

Some people think I still exist as the Abominable Snowman (a Yeti) or Bigfoot.

Procoptodon

I'm in this pouch to feed on my mother's milk and grow.

Scientists studying this huge ape's fossilized teeth think it probably ate bamboo.

Eosimias was tiny, weighing less than an apple. It probably ate insects.

Eosimias

Eosimias *may have been an ancestor of all modern monkeys and apes.*

What is an ancestor?

An ancestor is an early type of animal that has modern relatives. *Eosimias* was an early type of tiny monkey that lived about 40 mya. Ten million years later, a larger monkey had evolved.

Could a bird eat a horse?

Yes! Some early horses were as small as a pet cat. They made a tasty snack for giant birds.

Tiny Propalaeotherium could hide from predators in dense, shady forests.

Sifrhippus was about the size of a small dog.

Propalaeotherium

Sifrhippus

Why do whales breathe air?

That's because their ancestors were four-legged animals that lived on land.

Pakicetus

I lived by the coast and hunted on land or in the shallow water.

Look, no legs! I'm a whale and a great swimmer, but I needed to come to the surface to breathe air.

Dorudon

I'm called a missing link. I'm half-way between a four-legged land animal and a whale. I spent most of my life in water.

Ambulocetus

Merychippus lived in cooler times, when being big helped animals stay warm. It could reach one metre tall.

Merychippus

Between 1.4–1.8 metres tall

Modern horse

A compendium of questions

Why all the strange names?

I'm going to call you... Dave.

When scientists find a new animal they can name it after themselves or where it was found, use Latin or Greek, or make up a new name.

What was the biggest fish?

Leedsichthys is a contender for the award of largest fish to ever live – reaching at least 16.5 metres long.

Despite my size, I feasted on tiny plankton, like whale sharks do today.

Which frog could bite like a cat?

Beelzebufo was a prehistoric frog with a sticky tongue and a deadly bite. It could even kill baby dinosaurs!

I am also known as devil frog. I can't think why!

Yikes!

I can't quite figure out this cube puzzle!

Who has cube-shaped poo?

Today's wombats make little cubed poos, but fossilized poo found from giant wombats is round.

How did insects end up in amber?

It can take millions of years for amber to form.

Prehistoric insects were often trapped in sticky resin from trees. Under the right conditions, the resin formed orange stone, called amber.

Have camels always had humps?

No. Synthetoceras had a flat back, but two horns on top of its head and a Y-shaped horn on its nose!

Only males had this weird Y-shaped horn, and we probably used it in fights for territory.

Which cat was a copycat?

Miracinonyx! It looked like a cheetah, but was probably a type of mountain lion. It could run at 70 kilometres an hour!

When did prehistory end?

Humans began writing history around 5400 years ago — marking the end of prehistory and the beginning of history!

Munch!

What was the largest mammal to ever live on land?

Indricotherium was about 5 metres tall, but could stretch far higher with its long neck.

FOSSILS

What are fossils?

Fossils are the remains of living things that died a very long time ago, and have been preserved in stone. Next time you're at the beach, keep your eyes peeled. If you spot an unusual pattern or shape on a pebble, it may be a fossil!

What do they tell us?

Fossils help us work out how animals lived millions of years ago.

We can find out what they ate and where they lived.

Ammonite fossil

Trilobite fossil

Which ones might you find?

The most common fossils are of ancient sea creatures. Ammonites had spiral shells. Trilobites looked a bit like today's woodlice.

Ammonites were fierce hunters, related to squid. Some were almost as big as a car!

Which animals got fossilized?

All sorts! Creepy-crawlies, dragonflies, birds, fish, snakes, crocodiles. Most are are extinct — they no longer exist.

Coiled shell

Deinosuchus, prehistoric crocodile

Ammonite

Big eyes

Trilobites could range in size from a tiny grain of sand to the size of a basketball!

Tentacles

Trilobite

Hard exoskeleton

Could you find a dinosaur?
You certainly could! In 2021 a 4-year-old girl in Wales, UK, found the fossil footprint of a dinosaur at the seaside.

Dracorex Hogwartsia

Were fossils dragon bones?

Long ago, people thought that fossils were the bones of dragons or giants from myths and legends. Today, we know that fossils are the remains of animals and plants that lived long ago.

Raaaar!

Scientists discovered my skull in 2004. I look like a dragon, but really I'm a dinosaur.

Some scientists think the fossil skull may be that of another type of dinosaur.

Dracorex hogwartsia means Dragon King of Hogwarts!

Who were the first fossil hunters?

Mary Anning

About 200 years ago, people collected fossils and sold them to tourists. Mary Anning's family did this in Dorset, England. Mary became a famous collector and made many important discoveries.

i found this ichthyosaur fossil when i was only 12 years old!

i am Mary's ichthyosaur. i lived in the sea about 200 million years ago (mya).

What did Darwin say?

In the 1700s and 1800s, scientists, like Charles Darwin, realized that living things slowly changed, or evolved. They did this to adapt to the world they lived in. If they didn't, they often became extinct (died out).

Scientists who study prehistoric life are called palaeontologists.

79

How did animals turn to stone?

After an animal dies, its remains might become squashed into mud or buried underground. They can turn into fossils in various ways.

1 A dinosaur is attacked. It dies in a lake.

Most animals die in the wrong conditions to become fossilized...

2 Soft body parts are eaten by animals, or rot away. Bones, teeth and claws are buried by mud. The lake dries up.

3 Over the ages, many more layers of mud settle on top. They press down on the mud below until it hardens into rock.

...so there are many extinct animals that we will never know about.

4 Minerals in the bones are replaced by minerals in the ground. These turn the bones to stony fossils.

5 After millions of years, erosion exposes the fossil.

Do fossils form in other ways?

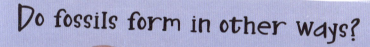

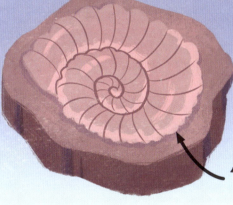

A cast fossil is made when an empty shape fills up with solid mud, which becomes stone.

Ammonite raised

Ammonite impression

A mould fossil is made when remains leave behind an empty shape pressed into the mud.

Yes they do! Not all fossils form from bone.

A trace fossil may be made up of animal tracks or leaf imprints left behind in wet mud, which later harden into stone.

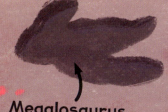

Megalosaurus footprint

How many!

The smallest dinosaur fossil found so far was just **40** centimetres long. Fossils of *Microraptor* have been found in China.

i was as big as a modern-day hummingbird!

Titanomyrma was a monster prehistoric ant measuring a whopping **5** centimetres long! Its fossils have been found in the United States.

77

The weight in tonnes of the gigantic dinosaur *Argentinosaurus*. Can you guess where its fossils were found?

The fastest dinosaur was *Ornithomimus*. It may have reached speeds of **80** kilometres an hour. Fossils of this bird-like dino have been found in North America.

2.2 The length in metres of a single sauropod thigh bone found in France! It weighed **500** kilograms!

12.8 The length in metres of the longest fossil snake, Titanoboa , found in South America.

My fossils were first discovered in Colombia, in 2009

Where can you search?

Fossils can be found in rock falls, cliffs, quarries and on beaches. They are easier to find if rocks break up, or get worn away by wind or water.

How can a fish end up on top of a mountain?

Earth's rocks are always on the move, slipping, sliding or folding. Layers of rock are pushed up and down. A fossil that was once on the seabed can end up on a mountaintop.

What is the fossil record?

It's the story of our planet, and it's under our feet. As millions of years pass, new layers of rock cover the older ones. Each layer is from a different age, and so it has its own fossil plants and animals.

How did I end up here?

Quaternary

Neogene

Paleogene

Cretaceous

Jurassic

Triassic

Cenozoic Era
66 mya–present day

Mesozoic Era
251–66 mya

Slate

Shale

Chalk

Limestone

Sandstone

Which are the best rocks to look for?

Know your rocks! Studying rocks is called geology. Good fossils can often be found in **sandstone, shale, chalk, slate and limestone.**

Permian

Carboniferous

Devonian

Silurian

Ordovician

Cambrian

Palaeozoic Era
541–251 mya

Earth's history is split into giant eras of time, which are then split up into shorter periods.

Have the continents moved too?

Yes, the continents sit on moving sections of the Earth's surface, called plates. So over the ages, they have also moved position.

The fossil record proves that Africa and South America were once joined together.

Always remember safety first.

Always go fossil-hunting with a grown-up.

What must you always remember?

⚠ Wear the right clothes and footwear.

⚠ Don't climb cliffs or old mine shafts.

⚠ Don't get cut off when the tide comes in.

⚠ Don't damage rocks or cliffs.

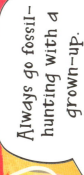

85

Did you know?

I was a small feathered dinosaur.

Microraptor

Some parts of the world are **fossil hotspots**. Liaoning in China has the most amazing dinosaur fossils.

Fossil beds are **NOT** where dinosaurs slept at night! They are large areas of land where there are **many buried fossils**.

Diggers or drills may be needed to clear the surface.

CLANG!

Scientists like to dig! They look for rocks of the right age, and search for any **clues** or fossil remains on the surface. They carefully plan the dig, **marking out the area into grids**.

Great care is needed when we reach the fossils. We use hammers, picks, files, scrapers and brushes.

Next, the fossils are taken to the **work room** to be prepared for the **laboratory**. This means **cleaning** away unwanted rock around the fossil itself.

Fossil embedded in rock

Electron microscope

Fossils are examined with an electron microscope – then the detective work begins!

Diadectes

When did the fossil **live**? What did it **eat**? How did it **move**?

Fossil fragments are pieced together like a jigsaw.

Tiktaalik

We could breathe air, and our fins evolved into legs.

Can jelly turn to stone?

Yes – in the right conditions! Sea creatures like starfish made they made good fossils because their body parts. Sea starfish because they had hard too soft. Jellyfish were their hard parts. Jellyfish sometimes imprints if their bodies left in silt or sand. But left imprints if buried in silt or sand.

Prehistoric jellyfish

Fossil jellyfish

How did fish go for a walk?

Some fossils from about 390 mya show fish that had special fins called lobes. They used these like fingers and toes, to squirm and wriggle their way onto land.

Why did some reptiles have flippers?

Reptiles evolved from amphibians about 320 mya. Some returned to life in the oceans. Fossils of plesiosaurs show that they developed flippers to help them swim.

Plesiosaurus

Diplocaulus

Dunkleosteus

CRUNCH

My fossils show I had jagged bones instead of teeth, and an armour-plated head!

I was an amphibian with an odd-shaped head. Why was it like this? No one knows!

Who liked the best of both worlds?

The amphibians! They evolved from fish about 350 mya, and lived on land and in water, like today's frogs.

I swam through the ocean hunting fish, which I caught with my long, sharp teeth.

Snap!

Who lurked on the seabed?

Meet deadly *Dunkleosteus*. This fish swam like an eel and was as long as a bus.

Why was the forest petrified?

Because it had turned to stone! Most plant fossils are pressed shapes, but some trees turn into entire fossils because of minerals in the water they soak up.

Petrified can mean terrified – but it also means 'turned to stone'.

1 Tree grows in a prehistoric forest.

2 Tree dies and is buried in mineral-rich mud.

3 Wood soaks up minerals, turning it into stone.

4 The fossil keeps the shape of the tree.

Arthropleura armata

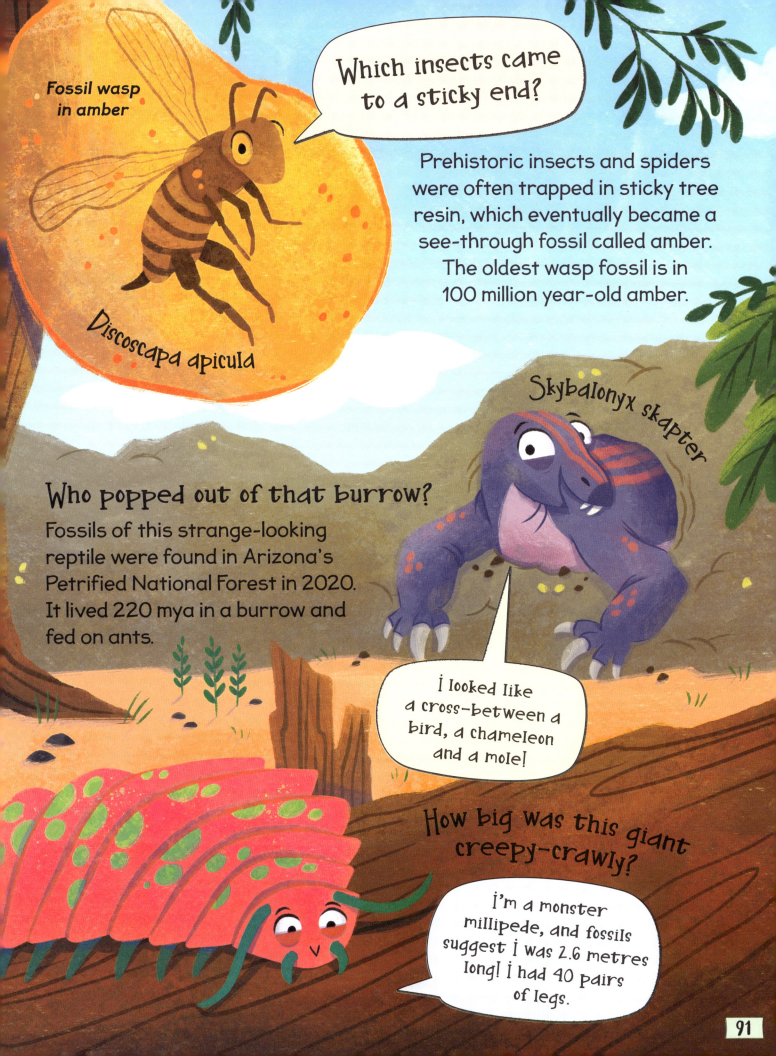

Fossil wasp in amber

Which insects came to a sticky end?

Prehistoric insects and spiders were often trapped in sticky tree resin, which eventually became a see-through fossil called amber. The oldest wasp fossil is in 100 million year-old amber.

Discoscapa apicula

Skybalonyx skapter

Who popped out of that burrow?

Fossils of this strange-looking reptile were found in Arizona's Petrified National Forest in 2020. It lived 220 mya in a burrow and fed on ants.

I looked like a cross-between a bird, a chameleon and a mole!

How big was this giant creepy-crawly?

I'm a monster millipede, and fossils suggest I was 2.6 metres long! I had 40 pairs of legs.

How do we know about dinosaurs?

Fossils tell us much more than what dinosaurs looked like. Scientists can work out what they ate, how they moved, how they behaved and even if they were good parents!

Long neck

Huge, slow-moving body

Patagotitan mayorum

The veggie lover

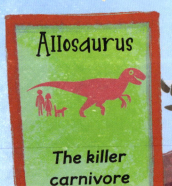

Allosaurus

The killer carnivore

My peg-like teeth were ideal for stripping and chewing plants.

Neck frill may have attracted mates

Long, sharp horns used as defence

My huge skull was almost 3 metres long, and I had a sharp beak for eating plants.

Triceratops
The sharp-horned beast

Some of my bones have scars and toothmarks. This means I got into a lot of fights!

Killer jaws and teeth

Eggs, nests and babies have all been found as fossils.

Deadly claws

Oviraptor
The caring one

I was found protecting my eggs from another dinosaur.

Fossil eggs can be scanned to show the babies inside.

Would you rather?

Find a beautiful **fossil fern** or a fossilized **shark's tooth**?

Live in a **prehistoric desert** with dinosaurs, or a **swampy forest** with ancient crocs?

Swim with the giant shark **Megalodon** or the squid-like tentacled **Tusoteuthis**?

Have a race against a lumbering **Stegosaurus** or a speedy **Struthiomimus**?

Meet a dagger-toothed **Allosaurus** in a museum or in real life?

ROAR!

Piece together the skeleton of a huge **Diplodocus** or a tiny **pig-footed bandicoot**?

Have a snappy **Heterodontosaurus** as a pet or an **Epidexipteryx** with long tail feathers?

Who is Sue?

Sue is the most famous fossil dinosaur in the world! It is the biggest, most complete T rex skeleton ever found and is named after Sue Hendrickson, the fossil hunter who discovered this giant in 1990.

250 of Sue's bones have been found.

Why is fossil poo so special?

Because poo gives valuable information about the eating habits of prehistoric animals. Scientists call fossil poo coprolites.

Coprolite

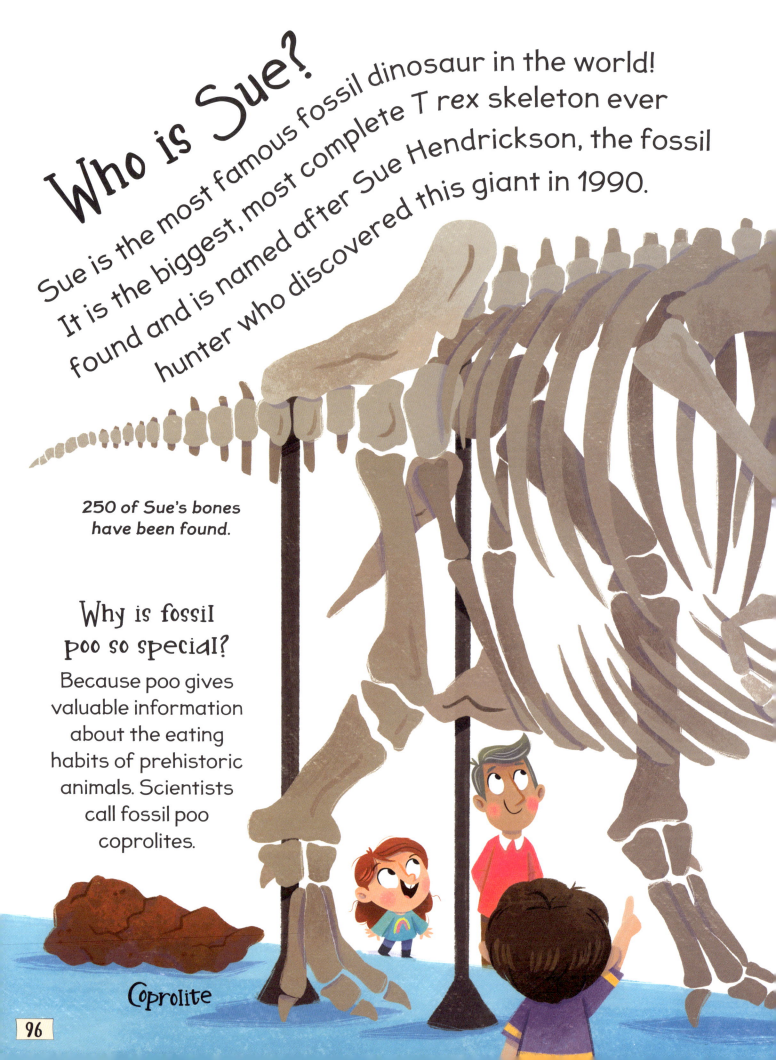

Can feathers be fossils?

We now know from fossils that many of the later dinosaurs had feathers or hair-like strands. These probably evolved from scales.

Feathers are clearly visible in this fossil of Sinosauropteryx

ROAR!

Ringed tail

Sinosauropteryx

Light and dark brown feathers

> I died aged about 28, and weighing 5.5–6.5 tonnes!

> Tiny structures in my fossil feathers suggest I was light and dark brown with a ringed tail.

Can fossils capture colours?

We're only just beginning to find out. Scientists are studying fossils to find pigments that colour skin, hair or feathers. These could tell us a lot about how animals lived.

Did dinosaurs fly?

No, but the pterosaurs did! Pterosaurs ruled the skies for 150 million years. They were cousins of the dinosaurs, but evolved the ability to fly.

Quetzalcoatlus

Who was the biggest flyer?

It might have been this pterosaur, known as *Quetzalcoatlus*. It had a wingspan of over 11 metres. Its 72-million-year-old fossils have been found in Texas in the USA.

Huge wings for soaring on warm currents of air

Long fourth finger

Toothed beak

Pterodactylus antiquus

Our fossils are rare as our bones were thin and hollow.

Which fossil is priceless?

This important *Archaeopteryx* fossil is. Found in Germany, it shows the links between dinosaurs and birds. It had reptile teeth but the wings and feathers of a bird. And it could fly!

Archaeopteryx

Birds evolved from dinosaurs. So the birds you see today are actually dinosaurs!

Where are the fossils of birds?

Fossils of true birds are very rare. To fly well they needed to have light, hollow bones. These were easily broken and lost.

Toothless beak

A fossil *Archaeopteryx* set in limestone.

Birds are descended from small, feathered dinosaurs.

WOW!

Who took over the world?

When the dinosaurs died out, one group of animals began to take over the world – the mammals! Warm-blooded mammals include dogs, monkeys, whales – and humans!

> My fossils are the biggest of any mammal ever found.

Paraceratherium

Filikomys primaevus

Who was a huge find?

A giant, hornless rhinoceros! *Paraceratherium* was a massive beast that lived around 34 mya, and was more than 5.5 metres tall and 8 metres long.

The first mammals were tiny. Fossils of this mouse-sized mammal were found in North America.

Who was found in a deep freeze?

This woolly mammoth! Being naturally frozen in ice is a type of preservation. Although not a true fossil, this baby mammoth died around 40,000 years ago. It is perfectly preserved, with fur still visible on its legs.

Baby mammoth, Dima

Darwinius 'Ida'

Primates like me developed into modern lemurs, monkeys, apes, and HUMANS!

My footprints were found in Laetoli, Tanzania, by Mary Leakey.

Grasping hands

Why is Ida special?

About 85–55 mya, a new group of mammals evolved known as primates. The most complete fossil primate ever found is Darwinius 'Ida'.

I was named in honour of Charles Darwin.

Fossil of Darwinius 'Ida'

Australopithecus afarensis

Whose fossil footprints are these?

They probably belong to Australopithecus afarensis, an early ancestor of modern humans. Footprints were left in wet volcanic ash about 3.7 mya.

Humans like us only turned up in Africa about 300,000 years ago, so we really are newcomers in the history of life on Earth.

A compendium of questions

Is that a shark tooth at the end of my tongue?

Are fossils expensive?

They can be. The most expensive fossil ever sold was Stan, a T rex, named after the palaeontologist who found it. Stan sold at auction for almost $32 million US dollars in 2020!

GRRRrrr!

What are tongue stones?

They're the fossil teeth of ancient sharks! Long ago, people found them embedded in rocks, and thought they were the tongues of dragons or snakes!

Who named the first dinosaur?

English churchman and fossil collector William Buckland did, in 1824. He studied a fossil jawbone and teeth, and eventually came up with the name *Megalosaurus*.

Lots of fossils of Maiasaura babies and eggs have been found at Egg Mountain.

Why is a mountain made of eggs?

Because it's packed with fossilized eggs and nests! This fossil site in the Rocky Mountains, USA, is a hotspot for dinosaur fossil eggs, babies and nests.

What are living fossils?

Plants and animals alive today that have stayed pretty much the same since they were recorded as fossils. This coelacanth fish is one of them.

My name is Diplodocus, but you can call me Dippy!

Who is Dippy?

Dippy the *Diplodocus*! This superstar fossil dinosaur has been on TV, starred in a film and toured the UK.

Which dino had horrible hands?

Deinocheirus did! Monster fossils were discovered in 1965 by Polish expert Zofia Kielan-Jaworowska and her mainly female team.

I still swim in the oceans today!

Deinocheirus means 'horrible hands'!

I'm pals with Charles Darwin you know!

Who found a giant sloth?

Charles Darwin did, in 1832! Darwin found fossils of this 3-metre-long monster in Chile. The sloth was named Mylodon darwinii in his honour.

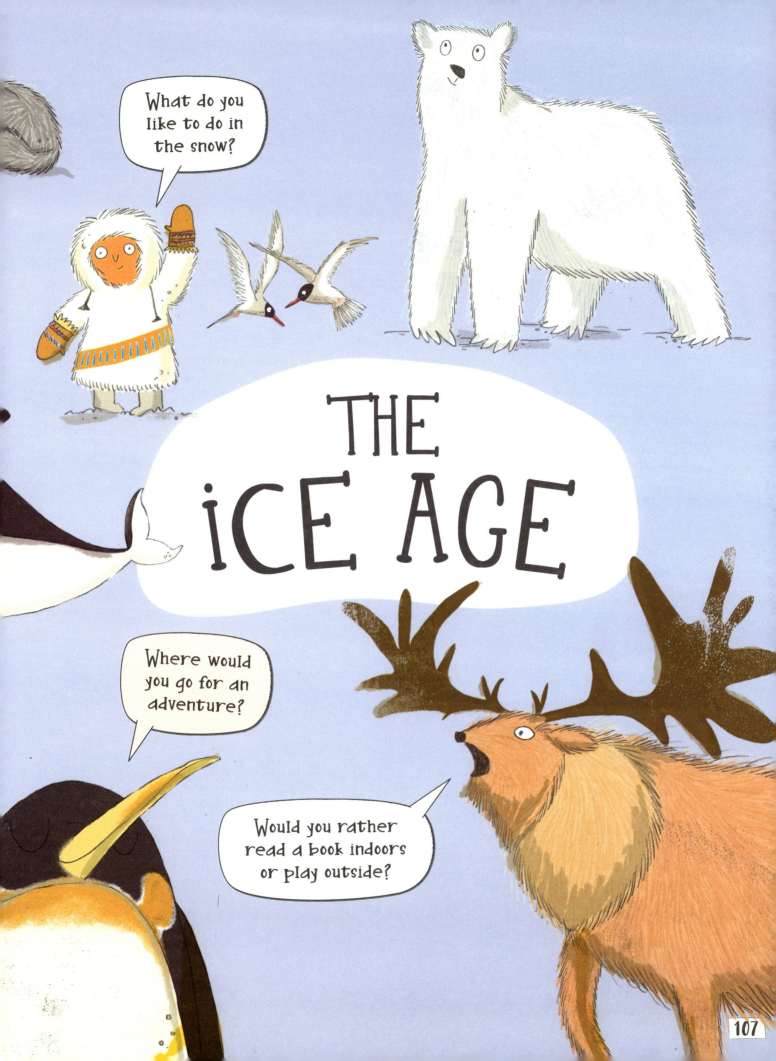

What is an ice age?

An ice age is a time when huge sheets of ice cover the coldest parts of the Earth. It can last for millions of years. An ice age affects the weather, and how animals and plants can live.

How old is the Earth?

The Earth has existed for about 4.55 billion years.

Snowball Earth lasted for about 120 million years.

Is that a giant snowball?

No, but it is a Snowball Earth! There have been at least five ice ages on Earth. During one of these, about 700 million years ago (mya), the Earth got so cold that it was covered in snow and ice.

ERA	PERIOD	EPOCH (MYA)
Cenozoic	Quaternary	Holocene 0.01
		Pleistocene 2.6
	Tertiary	Pliocene 5.3
		Miocene 23.0
		Oligocene 33.9
		Eocene 55.8
		Palaeocene 66

Earth's history is divided into chunks of time called eras and periods. Each period is then divided into epochs.

When was the last ice age?

We are living in an ice age right now! Our ice age began about 2.6 mya, at the start of the Pleistocene epoch. We know we are still living in an ice age because we have huge sheets of ice, called ice caps, over the North and South Poles.

We might have lived in ice age people's cave homes.

What animals live during an ice age?

Many animals that are alive today were around when the Earth was much colder, in the Pleistocene. Today's dogs, including Siberian huskies, are all descended from wild wolves.

Why does the Earth freeze?

The Earth gets mega-cold because of the way it moves around the Sun. Our heat and light come from the Sun – a great big burning ball of gases in space.

Sun

Sun's rays are strong.

Sun's rays spread out and have further to travel, so they are weaker.

1
The Earth is tilted as it spins around the Sun, so some parts get more heat than others.

One wobble lasts about 26,000 years!

Antarctic

ice cap

2
Sometimes the Earth's orbit (path around the Sun) changes and the Earth moves further away from the Sun, so it gets colder.

3
As the Earth moves it wobbles! The top or bottom can move further away from the Sun and get colder.

SOUTH POLE

Today, about 10 percent of the Earth is covered in ice.

NORTH POLE

Arctic ice cap

Sheets of ice are white, bright and shiny.

Reflected sunlight

Absorbed sunlight

How is ice like a mirror?

When sunlight hits an ice cap the light is reflected (bounced back to space) before it has a chance to warm the planet. This means that the world gets even colder and can stay that way for millions of years.

Where has the ice gone?

The Earth sometimes warms up during an ice age! Much of the polar ice melts before it flip-flops back into a mega-cold spell. This warm time is called an interglacial.

We are in an interglacial right now.

④ When these three things happen at the same time, our planet turns extra-cold and an ice age begins.

How many years ago?

2.58 mya– today
Quaternary Ice Age

3.6 mya
early human-ape

290 mya
Dimetrodon

251 mya
Mass extinction of about 90 percent of all species of animals

195 mya
Ichthyosaurs and plesiosaurs

150 mya
Brachiosaurus

66 mya
Another mass extinction saw the end of the dinosaurs.

300 mya
Meganeura

Jawless fish
415 mya

Arandaspis

360-260 mya
Karoo Ice Age

Ichthyostega

During this time 85 percent of all species were wiped out.

460-430 mya
Andean–Saharan Ice Age

479-206 mya
Orthoceras

366 mya
Early tetrapods

720-630 mya
Cryogenian Ice Age

2.4-2.1bya
Huronian Ice Age

380 mya
The beginning of tetrapods

Tiktaalik

420 mya
Land plants

800 mya
Simple sponges

mya = million years ago
bya = billion years ago

113

When was Earth like a greenhouse?

For most of Earth's long history, it has been a Greenhouse Earth. It is called this when it is very warm and there are no ice sheets.

Pterosaur

Aucasaurus

Buiteraptor

Did dinosaurs like it hot?

Yes! We thrived in the hot climate that warmed the Earth 100 mya.

Giganotosaurus

The dinosaurs died out when the planet's climate suddenly cooled down, about 66 mya.

Why do plants grow well in a greenhouse?

Plants need water, sunlight and a gas called carbon dioxide to grow well. There are lots of these things on a Greenhouse Earth, which makes it a perfect place for plants.

There were volcanoes erupting all over the planet 100 mya, putting lots of carbon dioxide into the air.

Argentinosaurus

What did your world look like?

There were enormous forests with lots of yummy plants for us to eat. Even the lands near the North Pole were covered with trees.

Plesiosaur

Why did the Earth get hot?

The air, or atmosphere, is wrapped around the Earth like a cosy blanket. When there is lots of carbon dioxide in the atmosphere it gets even hotter. It warms up the land and seas, and changes the climate.

What is ice?

Ice is frozen water. Water can be a solid, like ice, or it can be a liquid or a gas. When the temperature changes, water changes between these three states.

> Fluffy feathers trap warm air next to my skin.

Snowy owl

> We measure the temperature of water using a thermometer.

Gas

When liquid water warms up it turns into a gas.

Liquid

When solid ice turns into water it is melting.

Solid

When liquid water turns into solid ice it is freezing.

Liquid

← 100° Celsius Water turns into a gas

← 0° Celsius Water freezes into ice

How cool is ice?

Fresh water turns into ice at a temperature of 0° Celsius. Seawater has salt in it, and it needs the temperature to drop to about -2° Celsius before it can freeze.

How does snow turn into ice?

When water vapour in the sky gets very cold it turns into ice crystals and falls as snow. Layers and layers of snow build up and as it gets heavier the snow is squashed into thick layers, or sheets, of ice.

My blood is special. It doesn't freeze, so I am able to live in ice-cold oceans.

Icefish

We live in polar places where there is snow and ice.

Winter coat

Thick layers of fat help to keep us warm!

Summer coat

Arctic fox

Who changes colour in the snow?

Many animals that live in snowy places are white in the winter. This colour helps them hide in the snow. When the snow and ice melt in summer, some of them turn brown or grey so they can hide on the ground.

117

Did you know?

Hungry **polar bears** often lurk next to seal breathing holes. They wait until a **seal** pops its head up to breathe.

Seals use their nose and claws to break holes in the sea ice to breathe.

I'm waiting patiently!

Ice age mammals often have thick layers of fat, called blubber, to keep them warm. **Walrus** blubber can be 10 centimetres thick!

Colossal squid live in Antarctic waters. They can be 10 metres long and have the largest eyes of any animal.

An **emperor penguin** can hold its breath and dive 450 metres below sea ice to find fish and squid to eat.

Arctic terns raise their chicks in the Arctic but fly all the way to the Antarctic to feast on fish in the Southern Ocean. They travel 70,000 kilometres a year.

A **woolly mammoth's** fur was thick and long. Each hair could grow 100 centimetres.

An adult **woolly mammoth** needed to eat 180 kilograms of food a day in the summer to build up its strength.

I have a legspan of 25 centimetres!

Antarctic **sea spiders** can have eight, ten or even 12 legs!

Long daggers of ice, called **icicles**, can form when water freezes, melts, drips and re-freezes. The largest ones can be 30 metres long!

How big is an ice sheet?

Enormous! The ice sheets that make up the polar ice caps hold 99 percent of all the freshwater ice on Earth. Today, they cover Antarctica and Greenland but 20,000 years ago they were even bigger.

The ice sheets covered most of North America, northern Europe and stretched beyond Antarctica.

20,000 years ago

Today

Even today, the Antarctic ice sheet holds 70 percent of the world's fresh water and is 4.5 kilometres thick in places.

You might see a seal snoozing on an iceberg, or a seabird taking a ride!

Smaller lumps of floating ice are called bergy bits and growlers.

Why do polar bears love pancakes?

Polar pancakes aren't for eating! They are plates of ice that form on freezing water, especially in the Arctic Ocean. Polar bears use them like stepping stones.

Polar bears have been around for at least 4 million years.

How do you make an iceberg?

Icebergs form when big pieces of ice break off an ice sheet or a glacier, and float into the sea. An iceberg is at least 5 metres wide, but they can be much larger than that.

How slow does snow flow?

A slow-moving river of ice is called a glacier.

Glacier movement

Snow doesn't flow until it turns to ice... and then it flows very slooooowly. Ice sheets that grow on the sides of hills and mountains creep downhill, carving wide, U-shaped valleys into the rocks.

A woolly mammoth's tusks could be more than 3 metres long.

Woolly mammoth

Each molar was up to 30 centimetres long.

I snuffled around, using my long horns to dig into snow for the plants beneath.

Woolly rhino

What did woolly mammoths eat?

Like modern elephants, mammoths ate plants, especially grass and trees. Mammoths had huge grinding teeth, called molars, to mash the plants up and mix them with spit before swallowing the green mush.

Who had mega antlers?

Megaloceros did! Like modern deer, the males grew massive antlers to fight each other at mating time. These deer lived in forests and on the cold, wet grasslands that were covered in snow during the long ice age winter.

Megaloceros

I was an ice age member of the deer family.

RAAAR!

Smilodon

Did cool cats eat woolly rhinos?

Smilodon, a sabre-toothed cat, was a fierce predator. It stabbed its prey with fangs that grew to 28 centimetres long! However, woolly rhinos were so big that few predators — except humans — tried to eat them.

Would you rather?

Sleep for seven months of the year, like an Arctic ground squirrel, or **stay awake** for weeks at a time, like an Arctic tern?

What ice age meal would you prefer to eat – a **meaty stew surprise** or a **veggie hotpot**?

You would be safest with me!

Go swimming with a **polar bear** or a **Greenland shark**?

Investigate the ice on our **Moon** or **Europa**, one of Jupiter's moons?

Ski across the Arctic or **sledge** across the Antarctic?

Where would you rather be on 21 December — the **South Pole**, enjoying a 24-hour day, or the **North Pole**, spending the day in darkness?

SOUTH POLE

NORTH POLE

Have **hair** that reaches your knees, like a musk ox, or a **nose** that reaches your toes, like a mammoth?

Polar bear mothers spend the winter in snow dens, where they give birth to their cubs.

Dig a **snow den** or build an **igloo**?

125

Megalonyx

I could stand 3 metres tall and use my enormous claws to rip leaves from trees!

How scary was an ice age sloth?

Megalonyx wasn't a fearsome predator, but it still made a scary sight. This furry beast lived in forests until it went extinct, about 12,000 years ago.

Which ice age beast looked like a small car?

Giant armadillos, also known as *Doedicurus*, were built like small cars and the same size – 4 metres long! They had bony plates on their backs to protect them from attack.

Doedicurus

Were dire wolves deadly?

Like grey wolves, dire wolves probably hunted in packs. They were bigger and stronger than grey wolves so they could have hunted larger prey, such as hose-nosed horses and bison.

Dire wolf

We could snap a big bone in two with just one powerful bite!

Macrauchenia

Whose nose was shaped like a hose?

Hose-nosed horses are also known as *Macrauchenia*. They used their long necks and odd noses to reach for leaves in trees.

I can use the spiked club at the end of my tail to wallop anyone who gets too close!

Which ice age animals are alive today?

We live in the Arctic Ocean, which surrounds the North Pole.

Blue whale

Many animals that lived in the last ice age have survived. They now live around the Arctic or Antarctica because the cold, snowy climate suits them and their way of life.

Narwhal

Can polar bears and penguins be pals?

No, because they never get to meet each other. Polar bears live around the Arctic, but most penguins live around Antarctica, at the other end of the world.

Do whales sing?

Some do! It's dark in the Arctic for half of the year, so it's important whales can hear members of their family, even when they can't see each other.

Chirp!

Beluga whale

Humpback whale

I am also called a sea canary, because I sing so sweetly!

Whistle!

Orca

My tusk can grow 3 metres long!

We live in a family group, called a pod.

Is that a swimming unicorn?

No, but narwhals have a long tusk that grows like a giant unicorn horn! Their tusks are super-sensitive and may help the whales find food in the deep, dark water.

Did people live during ice ages?

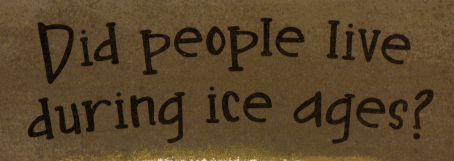

Humans have only been alive during the ice age we are living in right now. Life in an icy climate is difficult, as there are few places to shelter or find food.

Neanderthals had died out by 40,000 years ago.

There are many people who still live around the Arctic.

Denisovans were cousins of the Neanderthals. They lived in caves in Siberia.

Who hunted mammoths and bison?

During the ice age, modern humans lived in caves and hunted animals using tools that they made. Neanderthals also lived during the ice age. They were stronger, shorter and more suited to life in the frozen north than modern humans.

Who lives in the Arctic today?

About one million tribal people live in the Arctic, especially in Canada, Greenland and Russia. Their ancestors have lived in the bleak and snowy lands of the far north for thousands of years.

Many Arctic people follow ancient traditions and hunt or fish for their food.

Who looks after the reindeer?

Arctic people, such as the Nenets and the Sámi, herd reindeer and look after them. At the end of summer, the families travel with the reindeer, which go on long journeys south to reach warmer places for winter.

Is the world warming up again?

Cave bear

We are still in an ice age, but about 11,700 years ago the world began to warm up. The glaciers and ice sheets began to melt.

I went extinct. Today, humans are making the world warmer, so the glaciers and ice sheets are melting.

I went extinct when the world warmed up, but my relatives now survive in Africa's hot and sunny grasslands.

Why did ice age animals disappear?

Some are still alive today, but others died out because they could not survive in the warmer climate. It's likely that some ice age animals went extinct because humans hunted them for food and fur.

Cave hyena

How are we changing the climate?

Pollution in the air has extra carbon dioxide in it. This gas wraps around the planet, trapping the pollution and warm air close to the Earth. This is causing global warming.

> Solar power or wind power generate electricity without putting extra carbon dioxide into the air.

Who lives in Antarctica?

It's far too cold for humans to make their homes around the South Pole. However, scientists visit and work there for months at a time.

> We learn more about this special place, its climate and the animals that live there.

> We are using this weather balloon to find out how the climate is warming up.

How fast is the ice melting?

Polar ice is melting up to six times faster than it was 30 years ago. Melting ice turns into water and the sea level rises. This can cause flooding on land.

A compendium of questions

When did the Antarctic begin to freeze?

About 34 mya! But the Earth takes ages to cool down. It took more than 31 million years for the world to get cold enough for the current ice age to start!

During the last age, it was probably too cold, even for us penguins!

Do penguins like ice ages?

Yes, emperor penguins thrive in the Antarctic, where temperatures plummet below -30° Celsius. But they struggle to survive when it is colder than this.

Are sabre-toothed cats alive today?

No. Sabre-toothed cats went extinct in the Holocene epoch, when the world was warming up.

Pant!

We may have gone extinct because our prey became smaller and faster.

What is an 'ice mummy'?

Scientists discover the frozen remains of ice age animals when ancient glaciers melt. The ice preserves the body, including fur and skin.

How cold was it when
mammoths were alive?

During the coldest part of
the current ice age, the world
had an average temperature of
about 8° Celsius. Today, the
average temperature is
about 15° Celsius.

Brrr!

Do penguins live
in the Arctic?

No, but their cousins lived
there until about 220 years
ago. Great auks survived the
coldest weather of the ice
age, but humans hunted
them to extinction.

How do polar bears swim?

They do doggy paddle! Polar bears are great swimmers and use their enormous furry feet to paddle through the water.

My red 'balloon' helps me to attract a mate and warn rivals.

Who's blowing bubbles?

Male hooded seals blow a 'balloon' out of one side of their nose. It's big, red and made of their skin!

index